GREEN FILES

FUTURE POWER

GREEN FILES – FUTURE POWER
was produced by

**David West ** Children's Books

7 Princeton Court
55 Felsham Road
London SW15 1AZ

Editor: Gail Bushnell
Picture Research: Carlotta Cooper

First published in Great Britain by Heinemann Library, Halley Court, Jordan Hill, Oxford OX2 8EJ, part of Harcourt Education. Heinemann is a registered trademark of Harcourt Education Ltd.

07 06 05 04 03
10 9 8 7 6 5 4 3 2 1

ISBN 0 431 18290 6 (HB)
ISBN 0 431 18297 3 (PB)

British Library Cataloguing in Publication Data

Parker, Steve
Future power. - (Green Files)
1. Power resources - Juvenile literature
I. Title
333.7'9

Printed and bound in Italy

PHOTO CREDITS :
Abbreviations: t-top, m-middle, b-bottom, r-right, l-left, c-centre.

Pages 4–5, 7b, 8t, 9all, 12t, 17tl, 18, 30 - Corbis Images. 5t, 12b, 19t (Jorgen Schytte), 5b (Mike Schroder), 6t (Martin Bond), 11t (David Hoffman), 13t (Edward Parker), 13m, 14–15 (Hartmut Schwarzbach), 13bl (Hellier Mason), 13br (Matt Meadows), 15t (Jim Wark), 15bl (Joerg Boethl), 15br (Gerard & Margi Moss), 16bl (Mark Edwards 16br (Ron Giling), 17tr (Sabine Vielmo), 22 (Dominique Halleux), 23b (Roland Seitre), 24–25 (Arnaud Greth), 27m (Thomas Raupach) - Still Pictures. 6 - British Nuclear Fuels plc. 10–11 - Sasol Limited. 12tr - ARS/ USDA. 15m, 20–21b, 20t (Simon Webster); 24 (Frank Wilcox) - Rex Features Limited. 17b, 29b - NASA. 19b - Schlaich Bergermann und Partner Gbr/ Stuttgart. 21t - Professor Bryan Roberts & Team/ University of Western Sydney, Australia. 21b - Valérie Petitjean/ CITA. 25 - (Martin F. Chillmaid) Robert Harding Picture Library. 28, 28–29, 29t - EFDA - JET.

An explanation of difficult words can be found in the glossary on page 31.

GREEN FILES

FUTURE POWER

Steve Parker

Heinemann
LIBRARY

CONTENTS

The wind will blow for millions of years. This is the form of energy we are developing fastest, to generate electricity. Many shapes of blades, rotors or turbines are being tested.

INTRODUCTION

It's a cold, wet night. But indoors it's warm and bright, you've got a hot snack and good television. Suddenly there's a power cut or electricity 'black-out'. Everything goes off. Could such power problems happen more often in future? We generate most electricity today, from fuels that may run out tomorrow. We could use other forms of energy that are in endless supply, including wind, heat from the Earth and rays from the Sun. Otherwise one day the lights may go out – and not come back on.

Vegetable peelings, rotten fruit, garden cuttings – throw them in the digester. They decay to make a useful fuel gas, methane.

Inside Earth there are immense stores of heat energy. It's only near enough to the surface to be useful in a few places, like this geothermal plant in New Zealand.

Oil rigs provide fuel for power stations and also for cars, trucks and planes. Oil is adaptable, valuable – and running out.

'Power' has different meanings for different people. To a leader, it's telling others what to do. To a scientist, it's the rate of using energy, measured in watts. But for most people, 'power' is the same as 'electricity'.

OUR FAVOURITE ENERGY

Electricity is the world's favourite form of energy. We can generate it from many other energy sources, send it long distances along wires, make it strong or weak, and change it easily into heat, light, sound and movement.

Being GREEN

It's easy to save energy of many kinds, by using less electricity – which saves money too. Most new homes must be energy efficient, especially with plenty of insulation to keep in warmth.

Energy efficient houses, UK.

GENERATING ELECTRICITY

In most power stations, burning fuel boils water to high-pressure steam. This blasts past a turbine's angled, fan-like blades and spins them on a shaft. On the shaft are huge wire coils, the rotor. A small electricity supply makes these into strong electromagnets. As the rotor spins it generates much more electricity, by a process called induction, in the stator coils.

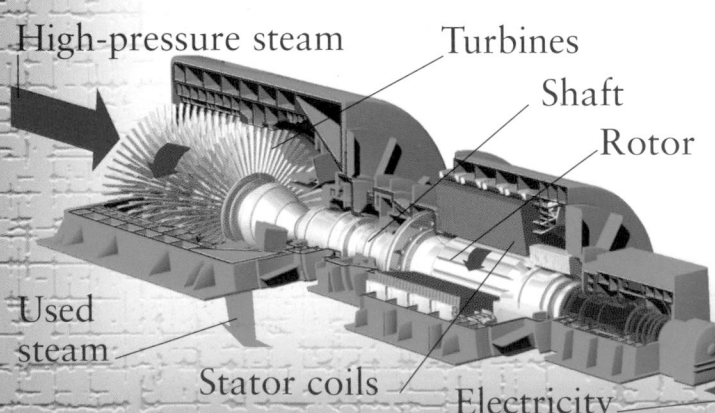

High-pressure steam
Turbines
Shaft
Rotor
Used steam
Stator coils
Electricity

Turbine room with steam pipes.

DIRECT AND INDIRECT

We use other forms of energy directly, like burning coal, wood or gas to keep us warm and for cooking, and wind-pumps that lift water from underground. Petrol and gas are also used directly for transport and heat. Electricity is an indirect source of power, because it needs other sources of power to generate it. About one-sixth of all the energy used in a developed industrial country goes to supplying electricity.

More than half a million big power stations around the world generate day and night, year after year, to feed electricity-hungry customers.

Worldwide, nearly two-fifths of all electricity comes from coal. Nuclear energy, from fuels such as uranium, also provides a vast amount. The only main energy source for electricity generation which is sustainable, long term, is moving water, for hydroelectricity.

NUCLEAR 16%

OIL 10%

HYDRO 19%

GAS 15%

Others 1%

COAL

Electricity is generated at large power stations and distributed to users. It is a massive operation both to generate electrical power and to make sure it reaches the millions of users.

CHANGES ALONG THE WAY

Electricity is generated as AC, alternating current. It flows one way, then the other, 50 or 60 times each second. AC has many advantages over DC, direct current, both at the power station and during distribution.

Most electrical cables and wires are made of the metal copper. Power lines use lightweight aluminium.

DELIVERING ELECTRICITY

Generators make AC more efficiently than DC. Also AC loses less energy as heat than DC, as it travels along power lines. Losses are reduced further by making it high in strength or voltage, using devices called transformers. DC cannot be changed by transformers.

Generators produce AC at about 22,000 volts.

Transformers increase AC to 400,000 volts.

Power station

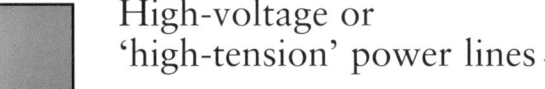

High-voltage or 'high-tension' power lines

Major electricity cables or power lines carry up to 400,000 volts (400 kV). At this strength, the current could leap through the air as a giant spark to an object nearby, and cause massive shock and damage. So the cables are held away from the ground on tall pylons.

Distribution control rooms monitor power station outputs and changing demands through day and night.

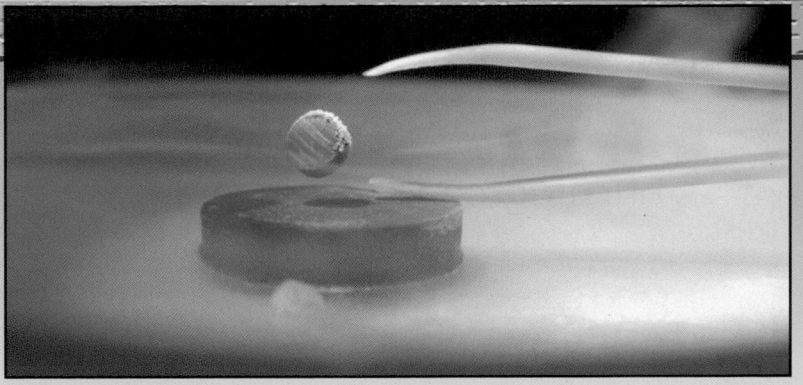

Scientists research a new super-conductor.

THE 'GRID'

Power stations are connected together by a maze-like network of cables called the electricity distribution grid. This has major power lines to towns and cities, where the electricity voltage is reduced or stepped down by more transformers, for daily use.

The enormous voltages of electricity in power lines set up strong magnetic forces around them. Some people say this can harm our health.

Power lines held above ground on insulated arms of pylons

High-voltage supply to industry

Main substation transformers reduce strength to 33,000 volts.

Local substation reduces to mains voltage.

Domestic mains supply of 110/220 volts to homes, offices, schools and shops

High-voltage electricity cables must be held away from metal objects or the ground by disc-like ceramic insulators, as in this transformer.

Fossil fuel reserves

2200
2100
2000

Coal   Gas   Oil

We are using up fossils fuels at a terrifying yet still-increasing rate. If this continues, known reserves of oil will be gone in 50 years, gas soon after, and coal in 200 years.

About two-thirds of the world's electricity is generated using fossils fuels – mainly coal, oil and gas. They also provide the energy for almost all powered transport.

WHY 'FOSSIL'?

Fossil fuels are remains of living things from ancient times, which died and were preserved in rocks. Coal is the part-rotted, squashed and heated remnants of ferns, horsetails and similar plants. Oil comes from the remains of tiny plants and creatures in the sea.

USED TOO FAST

Fossil fuels took millions of years to form. But we have used up more than half the world's known amount of oil in less than 150 years. However, oil and gas can be made from coal, which we have more of.

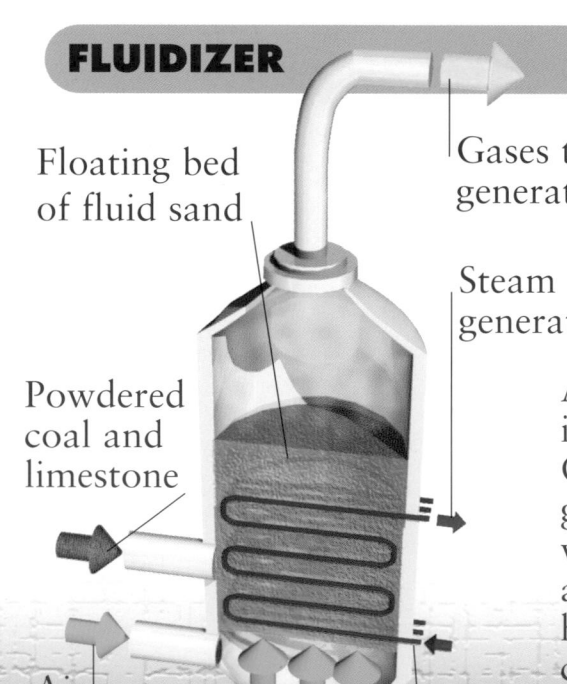

FLUIDIZER

Floating bed of fluid sand

Gases to generator

Steam to generator

Powdered coal and limestone

Air

Water

In gasifiers, coal can be 'gasified' by steam and oxygen, to make various kinds of liquid fuels and raw materials for industry.

A new way of burning coal is fluidized bed combustion. Coal and limestone are ground and fed to a furnace, where they burn in blasts of air, among sand that is so hot it flows like water. The coal burns more completely and makes less pollution.

Hot topic

Any form of burning makes carbon dioxide, CO_2. This 'greenhouse gas' traps warmth in the Earth's atmosphere, like glass traps heat in a greenhouse. It is causing global warming and possibly disastrous climate change.

Any burning or combustion, as in this power station, worsens the problem of global warming.

Burning fossil fuels is by far the biggest single cause of greenhouse gas emissions. Coal contributes most, and gas least.

CO_2 EMISSIONS COMPARISON
(kgs per Megawatt-hour)

900		
675		
450		
225		
0		
Natural gas	Oil	Coal

ARE FUEL CELLS THE FUTURE?

Fuel cells are similar to batteries, making electricity from chemicals, but their main fuel is hydrogen and they produce almost no pollution. Coal mixed into a soup-like slurry with calcium oxide ('quicklime') burns to release hydrogen which is used for the fuel cells. The heat also recycles the calcium back into its oxide. However another product is carbon dioxide, a 'greenhouse gas'.

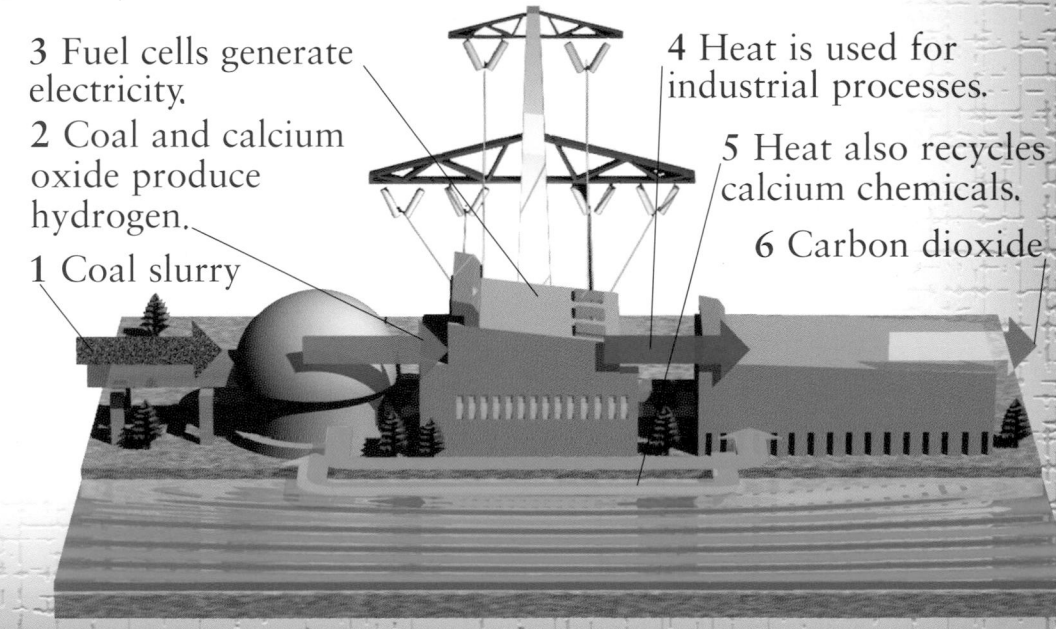

3 Fuel cells generate electricity.

2 Coal and calcium oxide produce hydrogen.

1 Coal slurry

4 Heat is used for industrial processes.

5 Heat also recycles calcium chemicals.

6 Carbon dioxide

The energy in fossil fuels like coal and oil came originally from the Sun. Plants trapped the energy in sunlight and used it to grow. Plants do this today, so could we use them as sustainable fuels?

ENERGY CROPS

Most farm crops are foods or are used for consumer products, like cotton. Energy crops are a newer idea. They capture sunlight energy and store it in their bodies as chemical energy. We can use this energy most conveniently by burning the plants or their products.

Maize (sweetcorn) is rich in high-energy oils. These can be added to hydrogen at high temperature and pressure, to produce burnable fuels like methanol.

ROTTEN BUT HELPFUL

Methane made by the biological or living processes of rot and decay (opposite page) is called a bio-gas. In the bio-digester all kinds of old plants, animal droppings, leftover foods and other once-living wastes decay and release methane. The rotted material in the tank is cleaned out regularly and used as soil fertilizer.

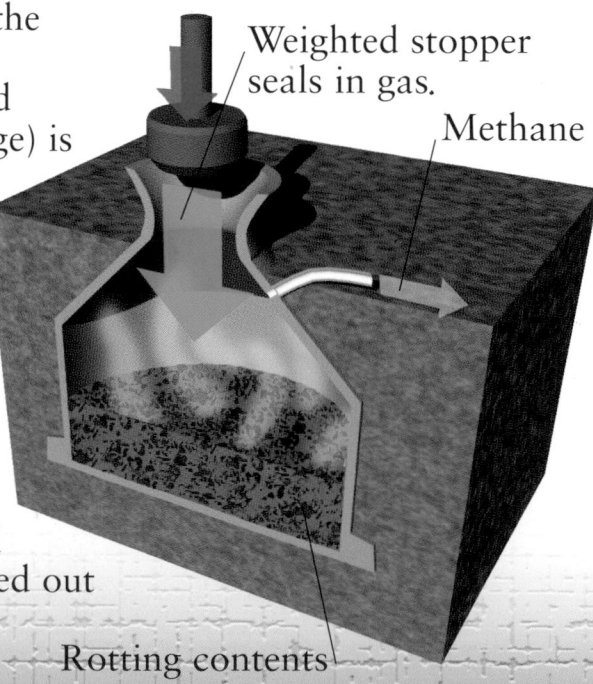

Weighted stopper seals in gas.

Methane

Rotting contents

Bio-digesters work well in warm countries like Egypt, where the heat encourages faster decay.

'Growing' alternatives to fossil fuels like petrol and diesel, are types of alcohol. They contain plentiful energy and are made in the same way as beer, by fermenting plant matter. They burn more cleanly too.

Brazilian motorists can top up with alcohol-based fuel made from fermented sugar cane.

MAKING METHANE

The fossil fuel called natural gas is largely methane. It burns readily and is a useful fuel. Methane and similar gases are given off by the rot and decay of once-living things, carried out by microbes such as bacteria. Bits of plants, animals and their products are rotted or digested to yield methane, for heat and cooking.

Modern life produces mountains of waste. This can be burned or incinerated as power station fuel (below). But the fumes may contain toxic chemicals and need cleaning.

Droppings are waste products from animals, but they still contain energy. This power station in Suffolk, England burns mainly a fuel made of chicken droppings.

13

About one-fifth of the world's electricity is generated from the energy of moving water. This is known as hydroelectricity. It is a sustainable source for the future, and it causes little pollution of the air. But it has drawbacks and limits.

ANOTHER SOURCE FROM THE SUN

Like fossils fuels, moving water gets energy from the Sun. The Sun's heat turns sea water to water vapour which rises high, condenses as clouds and falls as rain. As the water goes back to the sea, we harness its energy of motion.

The biggest hydroelectric scheme is the Three Gorges project on China's Ch'ang Jiang (Yangtze) River.

HYDROELECTRIC POWER STATION

In most hydroelectric schemes, water is held back by a dam. It flows under huge pressure along tunnels through the dam, and pushes against the angled blades of a water turbine. This spins on its shaft, which is connected to the electricity generator, as described on page 6.

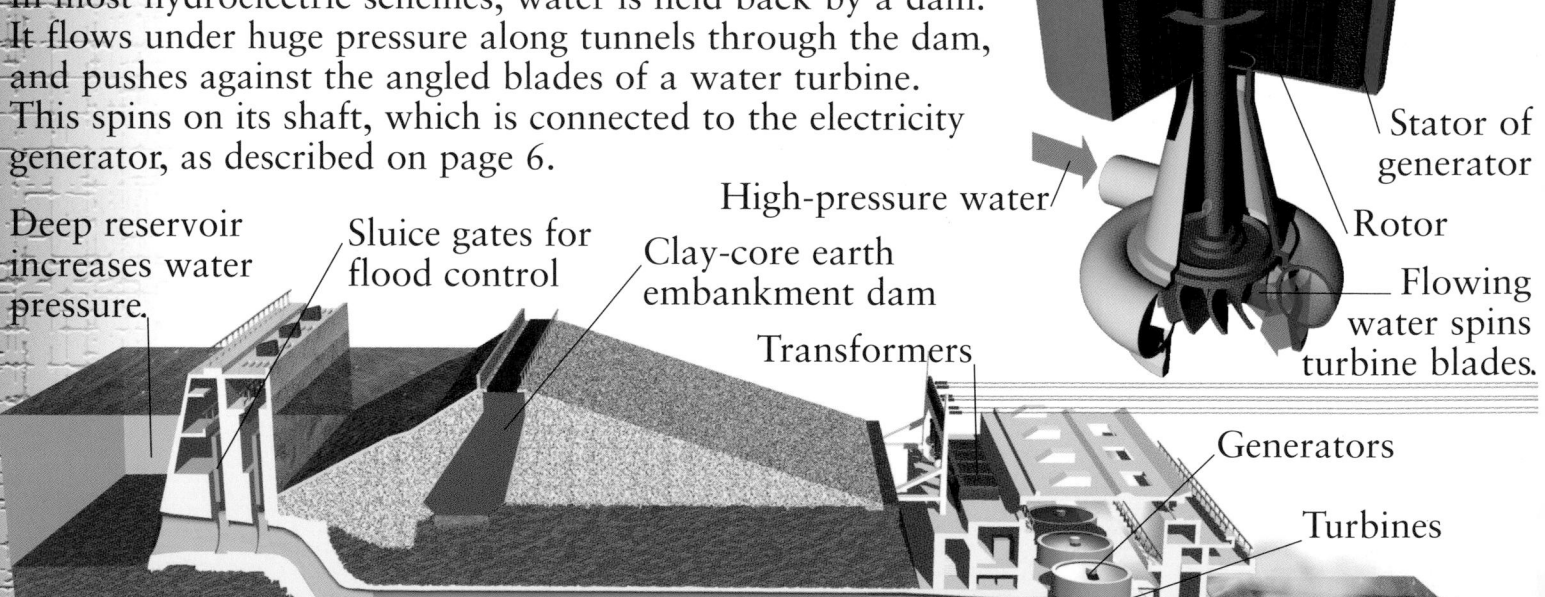

Deep reservoir increases water pressure.

Sluice gates for flood control

Clay-core earth embankment dam

High-pressure water

Transformers

Stator of generator

Rotor

Flowing water spins turbine blades.

Generators

Turbines

Steel-lined concrete tunnels

Water flows away along river bed.

In dry areas, rivers like the Colorado, USA, have so much water taken for crops or held by dams, they are barely a trickle.

DRAWBACKS OF THE DAM

Hydroelectric power stations are usually sited at dams. They hold back the water as a large artificial lake called a reservoir. This produces an even flow of water all year, and provides water for farm crops, fisheries and leisure activities like watersports. But as the reservoir fills, it floods valuable farmland and peoples' homes. Mud and silt build up, and river animals like salmon cannot travel to breed.

Hot topic

As a river rises behind a new dam, it fills its valley – and many people live along river valleys. In India, Egypt and Mexico, millions of people are being moved to new areas. So are some important historical buildings such as temples – or they are left to disappear below the water.

Drowned temple, India.

Rivers are major natural habitats, and some are home to rare creatures like river dolphins (inset). The massive Itaipu Dam in South America caused much disruption to wildlife.

SOLAR CELLS

We already use the Sun's energy from long ago, when we burn fossil fuels. But can we use the energy we receive from the Sun now, as it shines, by turning it directly into electricity?

MORE THAN WE NEED

Yes – but so far, only on a tiny scale. More energy reaches Earth from the Sun in one second, in all its rays and waves, than people use over the whole world each minute. But this energy is very weak and spread out, and it's much less when the Sun is behind clouds, and for half the time it's absent – at night.

A solar panel is a group of solar cells, which change light energy into electricity. Each has two semiconductor layers. The p-type tends to get rid of tiny particles (bits of atoms) called electrons. The n-type tries to collect them. Light gives the energy for electrons to jump between them, and this flow makes electricity.

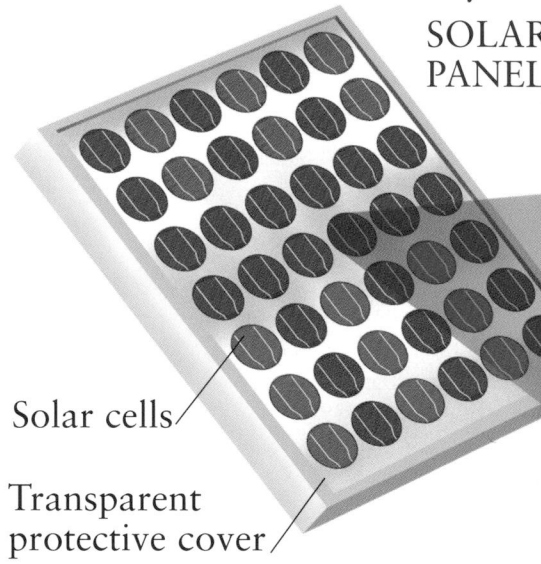

SOLAR PANEL

Solar cells

Transparent protective cover

Solar energy is helpful in remote places where installing electricity supply cables would be difficult, like this Bolivian hillside village.

Solar panels are costly. But once they are positioned in a sunny place, as here in Burkina Faso, Africa, they last for many years and need little care other than keeping clean.

An array of solar panels.

SUNLIGHT

SOLAR CELL

Electron-collecting wires

n-type semi-conductor

Electrons out

ELECTRIC CURRENT

p-type semi-conductor

Electrons in

p-n junction

Light striking the p-n junction energizes electrons to leap across.

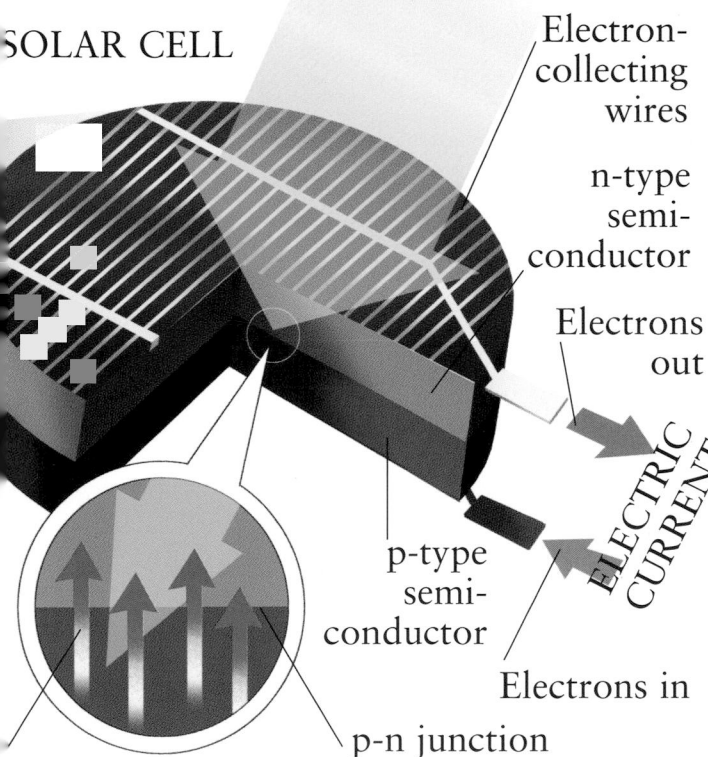

The Helios *group of light-powered craft include a car and a remote-controlled plane. They test new solar cells and help to make people aware of solar power.*

Solar cell factory.

CELLS AND ARRAYS

Solar (photovoltaic) cells are button-sized devices that change light to electricity. Each makes 1-2 volts, but many can be lined up in panels or arrays (groups), to produce enough electricity for villages. Solar power can also recharge batteries to produce electricity at night.

Solar (photovoltaic) cells turn light into electricity. But the Sun gives out many other forms of energy, including infra-red rays – usually called heat.

SOLAR WARMTH

The Sun's heat is difficult to change into electricity. It is so variable that the equipment needed would lie idle on cloudy days, in winter or at night. Solar heat energy is more suited to small-scale, local use – as heat.

The Sun's heat rays, like its light rays, can bounce or reflect off mirrors, and be brought together or focused into a small area, on tubes of heat-collecting liquid.

TRACKING THE SUN

The *Solar One* power station has more than 1,800 curved mirrors to track the Sun. They focus its heat on to a 91-metre tower, where a collector passes it to a heat-exchange fluid made of sodium. This flows along pipes into a boiler to make high-pressure steam.

Mirrors reflect Sun's rays on to collector.

Sun's rays

Collector heats fluid.

Hot fluid flows to boiler.

Solar One in California, USA. Boiler makes high-pressure steam.

Steam spin turbines.

Excess heat storage   Cooled fluid back to tower   Generator produces electricity

Solar energy of all kinds, especially light and heat, are most powerful and regular in tropical areas with little cloud cover. However the same hot, cloudless conditions make these lands near the Equator into deserts, where few people live or need power.

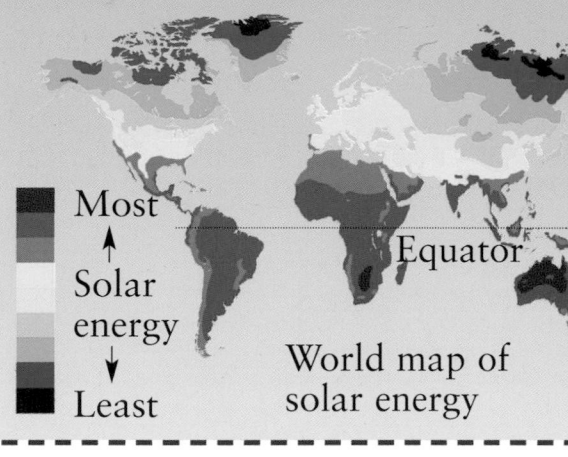

Most

↑

Solar energy

↓

Least

Equator

World map of solar energy

Solar-heated house, India.

A solar oven's curved mirror brings the Sun's heat rays together for cooking.

TAKING ADVANTAGE

One way of making the Sun's heat useful for when it does not shine, is cooking. Meals can be cooked to eat later. Another method is to store the warmth in huge tanks or ponds of water, to heat buildings during cooler times. However during a long, cold season, the warmth soon fades.

SOLAR CHIMNEYS

These are futuristic power stations with vast, low, greenhouse-like glass roofs, open at the sides. The Sun's heat warms the air and ground under it. Hot air rises as a fast-moving airflow up the tall chimney, which has a wind turbine generator near its base to create electricity.

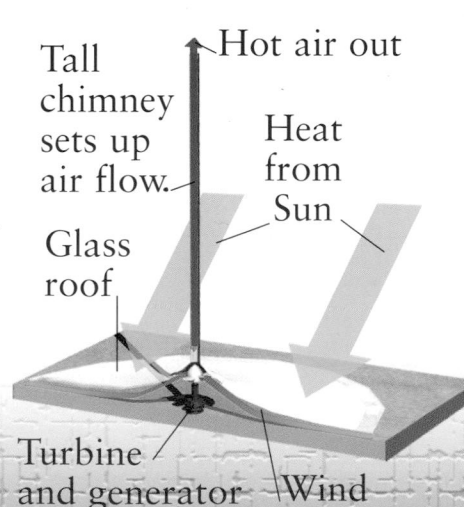

Tall chimney sets up air flow

Hot air out

Heat from Sun

Glass roof

Turbine and generator

Wind

Solar chimney for test purposes, Spain.

19

Most forms of energy on Earth come from the Sun – including wind. The Sun's heat warms some areas of air, land and oceans more than others. Warm air rises; cool air slides along to fill the gap; the result is wind.

Hot topic
Tall turbines have blades 100 metres long. Bu higher still, the winds are faster. A gyromill's blades whirl in the wind, both to generate electricity and kee aloft on the tethering cable This is wound in or out to place the gyromill at the most suitable height.

AGE-OLD ENERGY SOURCE
Like watermills in rivers, windmills have harnessed this sustainable form of kinetic (movement) energy for hundreds of years. The modern version, the wind turbine, changes air motion into electrical energy.

Windmills mainly ground wheat and other grains into flour for bread. On calm days, the miller did other jobs.

Turbines along coasts receive steady winds, uninterrupted by hills and valleys, but they may also be battered by ocean gales.

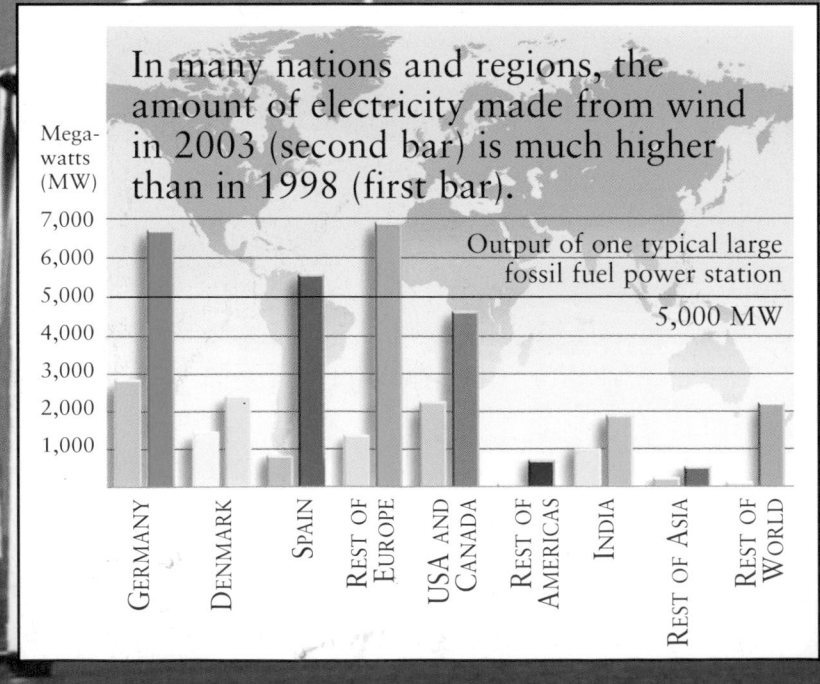

In many nations and regions, the amount of electricity made from wind in 2003 (second bar) is much higher than in 1998 (first bar).

Mega-watts (MW)

Output of one typical large fossil fuel power station

5,000 MW

7,000
6,000
5,000
4,000
3,000
2,000
1,000

GERMANY
DENMARK
SPAIN
REST OF EUROPE
USA AND CANADA
REST OF AMERICAS
INDIA
REST OF ASIA
REST OF WORLD

Like a kite, the gyromill stays high.

FOR AND AGAINST

Wind has benefits and problems. It will last as long as we can imagine, and once turbines are installed, they cause no air pollution or greenhouse gases. But build costs are high for turbines and they can be damaged by storms. They also interfere with the view, and can be noisy and even a danger to birds and other wildlife.

WIND TURBINE (AEROGENERATOR)

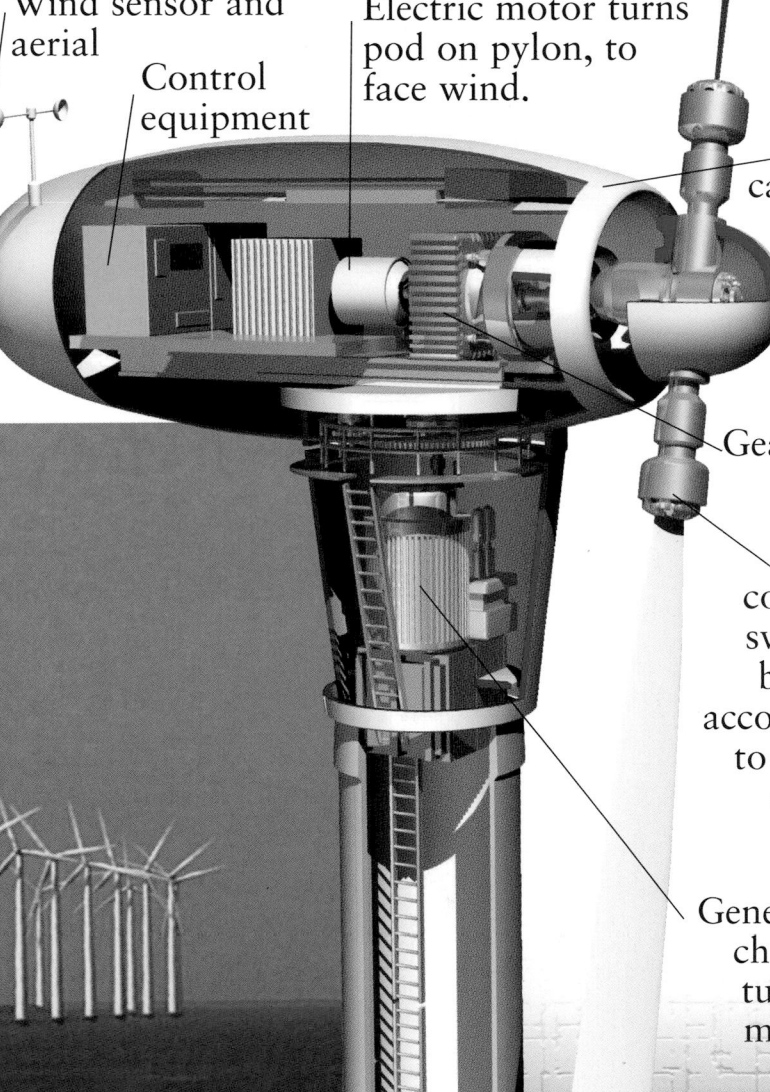

Wind sensor and aerial

Control equipment

Electric motor turns pod on pylon, to face wind.

Pod casing

Gearbox

Pitch control swivels blades according to wind speed.

Generator changes turning motion into electricity.

A typical wind turbine is housed in a weatherproof pod. Its blades (rotors) are clear of the ground, up where winds are stronger and steadier. Because of the way AC mains electricity is generated (page 8), the blades must rotate at a certain rate. As the wind picks up, pitch controls swivel them to keep the rotation speed constant. Sensors monitor wind speed, vibrations and other changes, and exchange radio signals between the aerial and local control room.

New designs of wind turbine are tested for strength and efficiency, like the 'shroud' type where the wind is channelled through a circular rim.

21

One of the basic forces in the Universe, is the pull of gravity. Earth's gravitational force keeps us down on the surface. Gravity also pulls water down as it flows along rivers, for hydroelectricity. Another way of using gravity is to harness the tide.

UPS AND DOWNS

As the Earth spins once daily, the Moon's gravity pulls the seas and oceans covering two-thirds of the planet, attracting the water towards it. This creates two tides (bulges) of water that travel around the Earth, useful for electricity (below).

Moon's gravity provides three-quarters of the force for tides. When it lines up with the Sun, the added pull gives extra-high and extra-low spring tides.

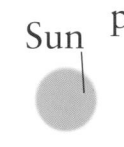
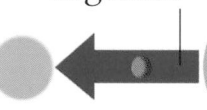

Neap tide

Gravitational pull

Sun

Moon

Pulls add together

Spring tide

TIDAL BARRAGE

The tidal barrage is like a hydroelectric dam across a river's estuary (mouth). As the tide rises on the ocean side, water flows through the turbines in the dam, into the river. As the tide falls over the next six hours, the reverse happens. The barrage is also a roadway.

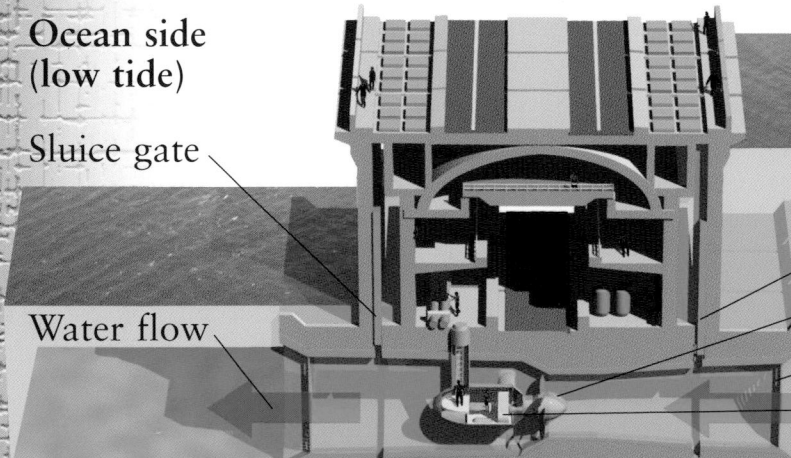

Ocean side (low tide)

Sluice gate

Water flow

Estuary side
Sluice gate
Turbine
Filter screen
Generator

There are two major tidal barrages with power stations, one across the River Rance in northern France (above), and a newer installation at Annapolis Royal, Nova Scotia, Canada.

WIND AND WATER

Waves are yet another source of energy to harness, which can be converted into electricity. This energy came originally from the Sun, via wind, which pushes water's surface into ripples and waves. A huge breaker crashing onto the shore contains massive amounts of energy – but this is partly a problem. Storm-force waves are very destructive, so wave-driven power stations would need to be exceptionally strong, and therefore costly. Yet in calm weather the generators might lie idle for weeks.

SHORELINE GENERATORS

Small seashore generators (below) trap wave energy 'second-hand', by funnelling each wave into a casing. This pushes air out of the casing, through a dual-direction air turbine, whose blades spin to generate electricity. As the wave recedes, air is sucked the other way. But the output is irregular.

Electricity

Two-way air turbines

Casing

Wave approaches

Wave recedes

NODDING 'DUCKS'

The Salter 'duck' uses large slabs that tilt to and fro on shafts, as waves pass. Their swivelling motion, like any movement, can be changed into electricity. Problems are varied weather and damaging storms.

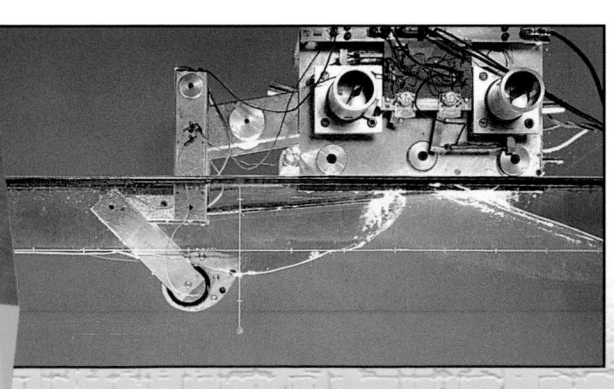

Salter 'ducks' bob like real ones.

Hot topic

Tidal power is long-term, sustainable energy. But the water flows along river and shore are altered, greatly affecting wildlife such as shellfish and industries such as fisheries.

Shores: home to bird life.

Earth formed over four billion years ago as a hot, rocky ball, and it's still cooling. Its heat energy will last as long again.

We can see the explosive energy from below ground, where we have fountain-like blasts of steam and hot water geysers.

DEEPER AND HOTTER

As we drill into the Earth, the temperature rises on average by one degree Celsius for every 35 metres of depth. This warmth is known as geothermal energy. It is immense, steady and sustainable.

GEOTHERMAL POWER STATION

One design of geothermal power station uses water to carry energy from the depths, up to the power station at the surface. The rocks far below are not only very hot, they are also under great pressure. As the water boils, this pressure helps to raise its temperature to form super-heated steam, which blasts up pipes to turn the turbines of the generators.

Steam is piped to surface and spins turbines.

Water is super-heated into high-pressure steam.

Power station

Cooled water from power station is pumped back down.

Deep rocks under tremendous temperature and pressure

Iceland is cold, but heating costs are low, due to cheap electricity provided by geothermal plants.

HOT WATER ON TAP

Geothermal or 'ground heat' energy is used in many ways. Power stations convert it to electricity, which can be transported long distances. Near the source, the heat can be used directly to warm homes, buildings and their hot water supplies. Greenhouses are also heated – bananas and melons grow near the Arctic Circle.

Many buildings like this Icelandic weather station use geothermal springs to provide heating directly.

Hot topic

Geothermal energy is growing fast in regions with hot rocks near the surface. These areas (red on the map) also tend to be unstable parts of the Earth's outer layer, or crust, and are prone to earthquakes and volcanoes. As rocks shift and crack, they can disrupt geothermal pipes.

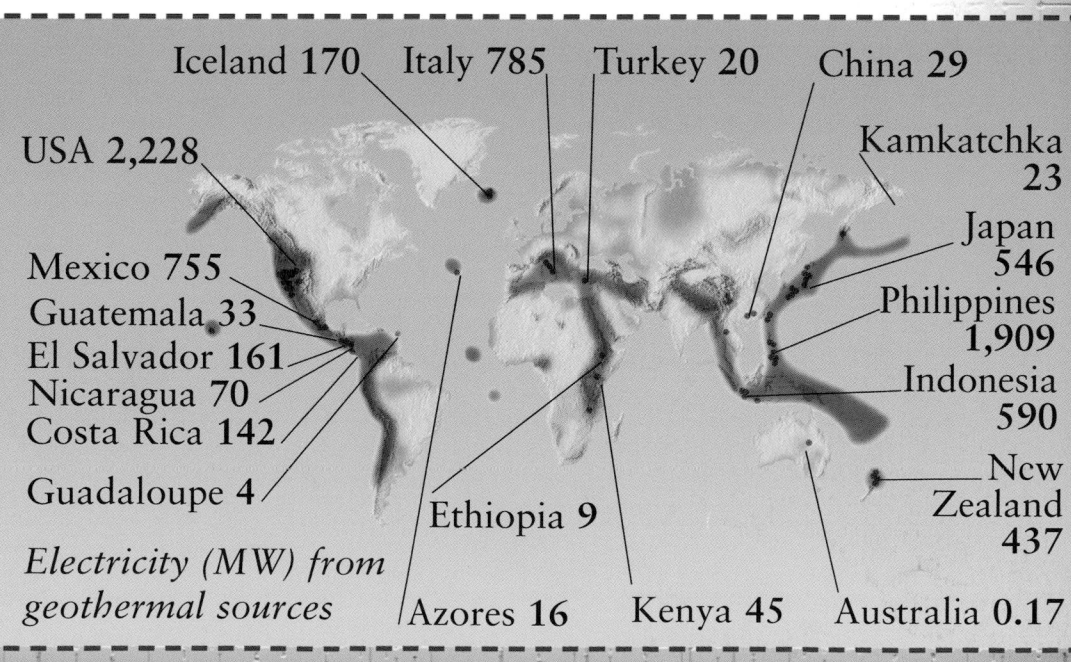

Iceland 170   Italy 785   Turkey 20   China 29

USA 2,228

Kamkatchka 23

Japan 546

Philippines 1,909

Indonesia 590

Mexico 755
Guatemala 33
El Salvador 161
Nicaragua 70
Costa Rica 142

Guadaloupe 4

Ethiopia 9

New Zealand 437

Electricity (MW) from geothermal sources

Azores 16   Kenya 45   Australia 0.17

Nuclear energy comes from the central parts, or nuclei, of atoms – the tiniest particles which make up substances. It does not involve burning, so it produces no greenhouse gases. But ...

RADIOACTIVE POLLUTION

Nuclear energy comes from splitting, or fission, of atoms in fuels such as uranium. It produces dangerous radioactivity which can harm and kill living things, unless carefully contained.

The reactor vessel must withstand incredible temperatures and keep in radioactivity. The fission process is adjusted by moving control rods in and out of the core.

NUCLEAR POWER STATION

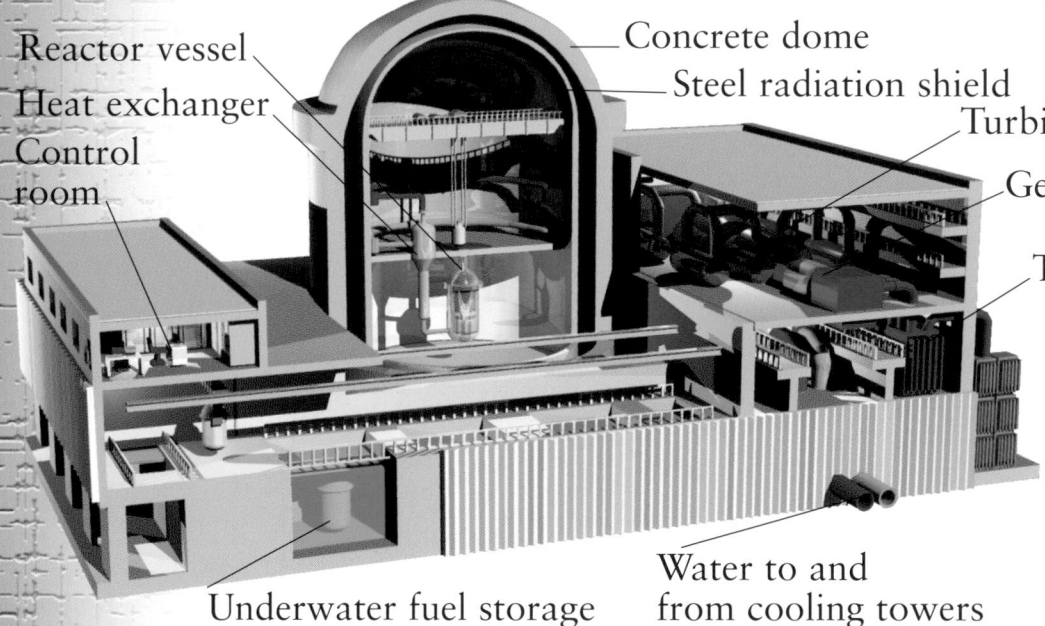

Reactor vessel
Heat exchanger
Control room

Concrete dome
Steel radiation shield
Turbines
Generators
Transformers

Underwater fuel storage

Water to and from cooling towers

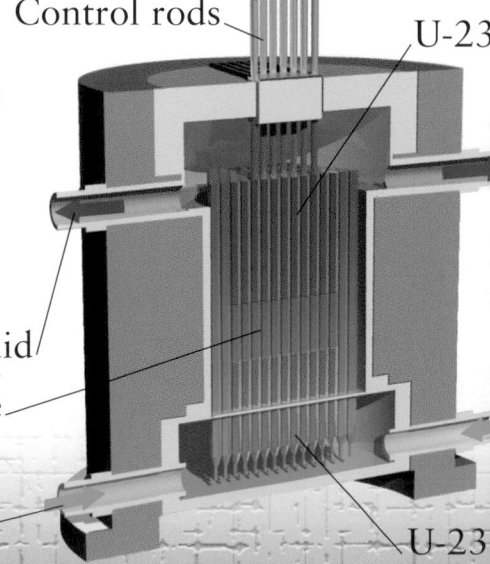

Control rods
U-23

Hot heat exchange fluid
Pu-239 core
Cool heat exchange fluid

U-238

In a nuclear power station, the heat source to boil water or the heat exchange fluid comes from radioactive fuel in the reactor vessel. In the type called a fast-breeder (right), the main fuel is plutonium-239. As its nuclei split, they give off heat, and they also change uranium-238 into plutonium-239, so 'breeding' more fuel.

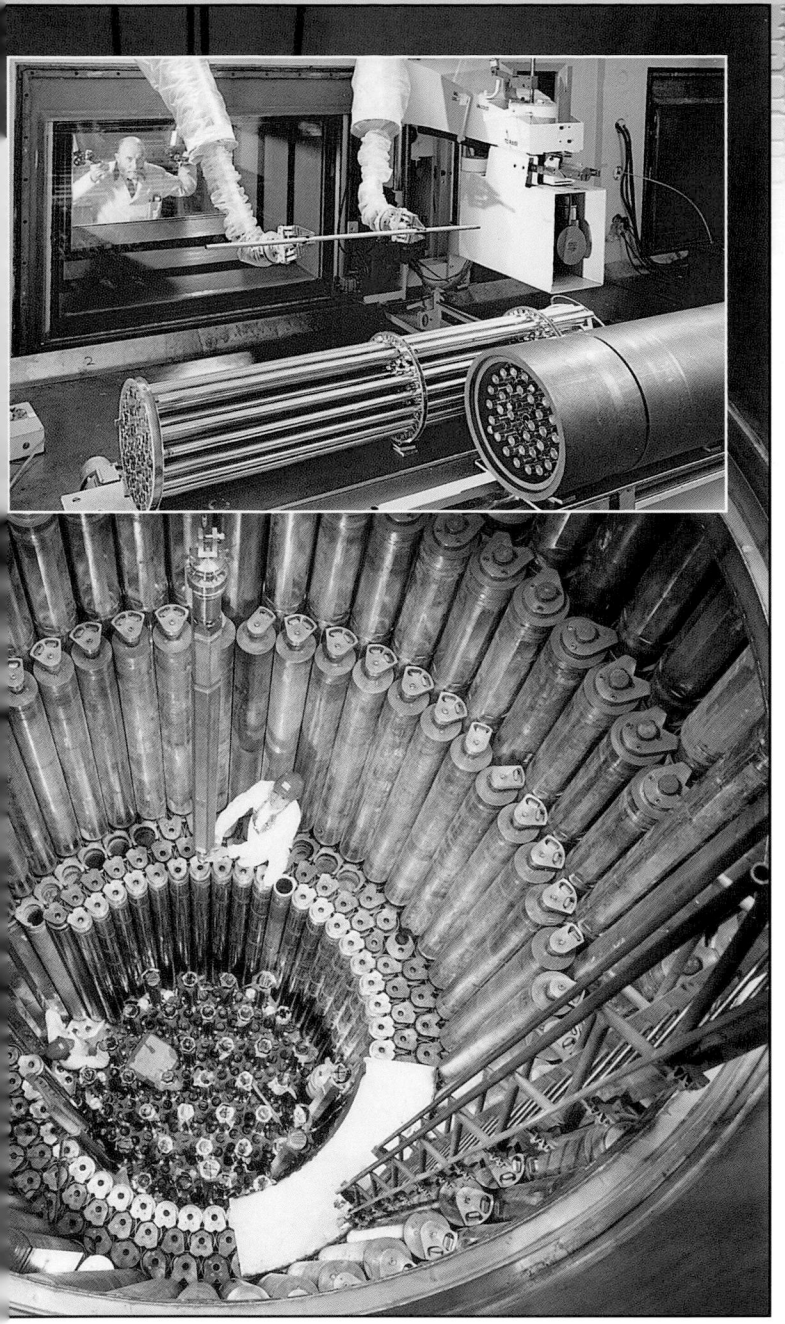

Hot topic

For now, spent fuel and equipment from the nuclear industry can only be stored in relatively safe places like old mines. But there is always the threat of a nuclear accident, or terrorists who might steal high-level radioactive material to make a 'dirty bomb'.

Nuclear waste stored in mines, Germany.

SAFER REACTORS?

Nuclear reactors are housed in a double-dome of steel and concrete, to contain any radioactivity which might leak within. But the risks remain of a terrible disaster, like the explosion at Chernobyl, Ukraine in 1986. In the proposal below, if the reactor becomes faulty it is flooded by water rich in boron, which slows and stops fission.

FUTURE POLLUTION

Radioactivity from nuclear fission is taken up in various amounts by all kinds of materials, equipment and fluids at the power station, even workers' clothing. Some items will be dangerously radioactive for thousands of years. There is no way at present of making them safe.

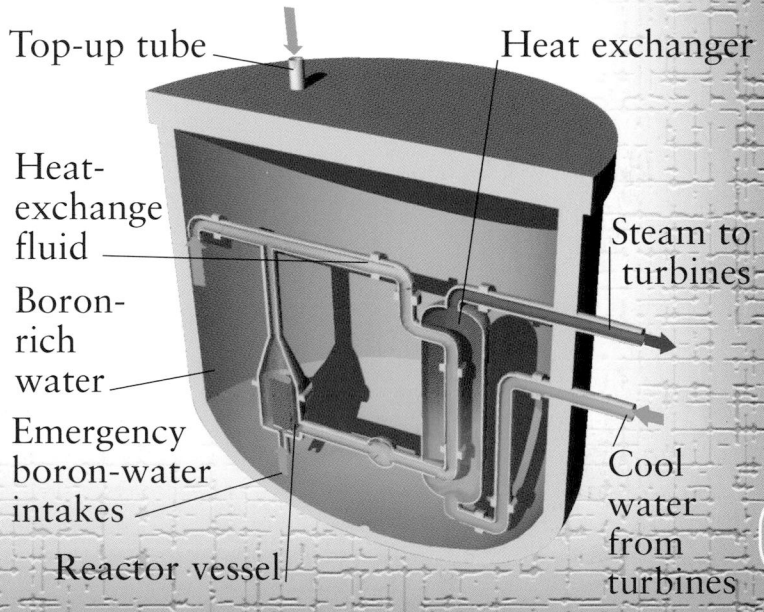

Top-up tube

Heat exchanger

Heat-exchange fluid

Boron-rich water

Emergency boron-water intakes

Reactor vessel

Steam to turbines

Cool water from turbines

27

Scientists continually search for new forms of energy, to use directly and to convert into electrical power. But some people do not want change just yet.

EASY LIFE – FOR NOW

Fossil fuels such as oil and gas are running out. However these industries pay the wages of millions of people, and make great profits for some. Our world teems with vehicles, ships and planes that run on fossil fuels, and which are familiar and convenient. New forms of energy and power could change all this.

Inside the fusion reactor, the plasma (see below) becomes incredibly hot.

FISSION OR FUSION?

In today's nuclear power, nuclei in fuel atoms undergo splitting or fission. This produces heat but also radioactivity. The opposite is fusion power, where nuclei join or fuse. It also releases heat and high-energy particles such as neutrons, but much less radioactivity. Substances used in test fusion reactors are forms of the gas hydrogen, deuterium and tritium.

Heat exchange fluid

Plasma space

Plasma outlet

Fuel inlet

Inner ring of magnets

Outer ring of magnets

FISSION

Uranium nucleus hit by neutron.

Nucleus splits.

More neutrons released.

FUSION

Deuterium (H-2)

Nuclei fuse.

Neutron released.

Tritium (H-3)

This plasma would melt the walls and so it floats in a magnetic field.

FUSION REACTOR

A fusion reactor is shaped like a hollow doughnut. Its fuel atoms are heated so much, they fall apart and are no longer gases but another form of matter, called plasma. As their nuclei fuse, this releases heat and also high-energy particles that continue the process as a 'chain reaction'. Several test fusion reactors have been built and run. But at present far more energy is put in, to heat the plasma, contain it and start the chain reaction, than comes out as heat to generate electricity.

FUSION FURNACES

One idea for the future is fusion power, which joins atoms rather than splitting them. A form of fusion power happens in stars such as our Sun. If it could be copied here on Earth, it might be similar to the nuclear power of today, but with much less radioactive pollution. However results so far, with test reactors, have been disappointing.

Hot topic

Energy from the Sun is much stronger and more constant high above Earth, in space. One suggestion is giant solar panels, bigger than sports pitches, to turn sunlight into electricity. Taken up in pieces by space shuttles, these panels would stay clean and safe for centuries. But the problem is transferring the energy down to Earth. High-power microwave beams are being tested, but if they hit the wrong place – BANG!

Artist's concept of a future space power station.

Electricity seems set to stay as our favourite form of energy, for many years to come. But the search is on for better ways of making it.

MORE AND LESS

As fossil fuels run out, electrical power must come from 'cleaner and greener' energy sources which are sustainable into the distant future, such as sunlight, wind, geothermal, tides and waves. Everyone can help. Try to raise awareness of these future power alternatives in your school, by designing a poster for display in your classroom.

Addresses and websites for further information

CENTRE FOR ALTERNATIVE TECHNOLOGY
Machynlleth,
Powys,
SY20 9AZ
www.cat.org.uk/
Tel 01654 705950
CAT is an environmental charity which focuses on renewable energy.

FRIENDS OF THE EARTH
26-28 Underwood Street,
London,
N1 7JQ
Tel 020 7490 1555
Fax 020 7490 0881
www.foe.co.uk
The largest international network of environmental groups in the world, campaigning to save energy in all forms.

GREENPEACE UK
Canonbury Villas,
London,
N1 2PN
Tel 020 7865 8100
Fax 020 7865 8200
E-mail
info@uk.greenpeace.org
www.greenpeace.org.uk
Powerful campaigning organization who take action against those who waste energy or refuse to switch to renewable energy sources.

AUSTRALIAN GREENHOUSE OFFICE
GPO Box 621,
Canberra ACT 2601,
Australia
Tel.1800 130 606
Fax 02 9274 1390
www.greenhouse.gov.au

ENCYCLOPEDIA OF THE ATMOSPHERIC ENVIRONMENT
www.docm.mmu.ac.uk/ aric/eae/Sustainability/ Younger/Energy.html
Huge website with detailed information on many aspects of future power and sustainable energy.

ENERGY SAVING TRUST (EST)
www.est.org.uk/
A non-profit company set up by the UK Government after the 1992 Rio Earth Summit, with major energy companies, working towards the sustainable and efficient use of energy.

NATIONAL WIND POWER
Riverside House,
Meadowbank,
Furlong Road,
Bourne End,
Bucks,
SL8 5AJ
Tel: 01628 532300
http://www.natwindpower .co.uk/
Leading wind farm developer.

UK SOLAR ENERGY SOCIETY
c/o School of Technology,
Oxford Brookes University
Headington Campus,
Gipsy Lane,
Oxford,
OX3 0BP
Tel 01865 484 367
www.thesolarline.com
A non-profit organization, mainly for adults, but with lots of detailed information, for all those interested in advancing our use of the Sun's energy.

GLOSSARY

alternating current (AC)

Electricity that changes its direction of flow 50 or 60 times each second. The mains electricity in houses and other buildings is AC.

direct current (DC)

Electricity that flows steadily in one direction. The most familiar form of DC is electricity from batteries.

energy

An ability to cause change or make something happen. It has many forms such as electricity, sound, heat, light, motion or chemicals.

generator

A machine that turns the energy of movement, usually spinning or rotating, into electricity.

greenhouse gases

Gases that help to trap heat from the Sun in the atmosphere, in the same way that glass traps heat in a greenhouse. They cause the overall temperature of the Earth to rise.

hydroelectricity

Electrical power that is generated from the energy of running water, usually by a power station positioned on a dam built across a river.

reservoir

An artificial or man-made lake, usually where water piles up in the river valley behind a dam.

solar

To do with the Sun.

sustainable

A process or substance that can continue for a very long time.

transformer

An electrical device that alters the voltage or 'pushing strength' (potential difference) of electricity.

watts

Units for measuring electrical and other forms of power. Megawatts (MW) are one million watts.